Saint Francis of Assisi

A Life of Joy

Written by

Robert F. Kennedy, Jr.

Illustrated by

Dennis Nolan

Sky Pony Press
New York

To Ena Bernard, who by her example, has taught my family all the virtues of Saint Francis

—R. F. K., Jr.

To Jan Baudendistel, who for eight years taught my daughter with understanding, joy, and love

—D. N.

Box Set Edition 2026

Sky Pony Press books may be purchased in bulk at special discounts for sales promotion, corporate gifts, fund-raising, or educational purposes. Special editions can also be created to specifications. For details, contact the Special Sales Department, Sky Pony Press, 307 Fifth Avenue, 4th Floor, New York, NY 10016 or info@skyhorsepublishing.com.

Sky Pony ® is a registered trademark of Skyhorse Publishing, Inc.®, a Delaware corporation.

Visit our website at www.skyponypress.com.
10 9 8 7 6 5 4 3 2 1

Library of Congress Cataloging-in-Publication Data is available on file.

Cover design by Kai Texel
Cover illustration by Dennis Nolan

Print ISBN: 978-1-5107-8682-0
E-Book ISBN: 978-1-5107-7912-9

Manufactured in China, January 2026
This product conforms to CPSIA 2008

Author's Note

SAINT FRANCIS, for whom my father and I were named, was a kind of patron saint for my family. My first memory—I was one year old—is of sitting below a statue of Saint Francis with my father's black Lab, Charcoal, in the garden of the Georgetown home where I was born.

The next year we moved to Hickory Hill in the farm country of northern Virginia. Franciscan iconography decorated our home, and the garden bristled with shrines and statuary celebrating Francis and his friars.

As a born animal lover and the saint's namesake, I felt a special affinity for Francis. My bedroom walls sported more than forty framed pictures portraying events from his life. My mother and father read us stories of the "little flowers"—the followers of Saint Francis, whose devotion to God and His creation gave them a special relationship with the animals. Theirs were the primary virtues—courage, sacrifice, generosity, and love for the poor—that my parents sought to instill in their eleven children. I read every book I could about these noble men who embraced humility and poverty, served the vulnerable and sick, gave their lives joyfully in martyrdom, and saw every hardship as a gift from God.

Francis continues to be an important part of my life. My own garden in Mount Kisco, New York, has two shrines to Saint Francis. His stories line my bookshelf and scenes from his life adorn my office walls. I often visit Graymoor, the Franciscan monastery at Garrison, New York, for spiritual retreats. Just as when I was a boy, my prayers to Saint Francis are invariably answered.

Every night my wife and I kneel with our children around the bed to recite the prayer of Saint Francis together.

Lord, make me an instrument of your peace.
Where there is hatred, let me sow love;
where there is injury, pardon;
where there is doubt, faith;
where there is despair, hope;
where there is darkness, light;
where there is sadness, joy.

O Divine Master, grant that I may not so much seek
to be consoled as to console;
to be understood as to understand;
to be loved as to love.

For it is in giving that we receive;
it is in pardoning that we are pardoned;
and it is in dying that we are born to eternal life.

Francis understood that we need to love nature and spend time in it, because it is through His creation that the Creator communicates to us His grace and joy. Just as we know Michelangelo by looking at the Sistine Chapel, we know God best by looking at His masterpieces. And His finest work, arguably, was the little saint from Assisi, whose single aspiration was that his life be the perfect imitation of Christ's. After Saint Mary, Saint Francis remains the most popular saint in Christendom. He is also an ecumenical saint; even in his lifetime, he was praised as holy by both Christians and Muslims.

There are many wonderful stories of Saint Francis that I've left out of the book, and hundreds more about his followers: his extraordinary meeting, during the Crusades, with the sultan, who recognized Francis as a holy man; his reception of the stigmata of Christ, the bleeding holes in his hands, feet, and side that he would bear painfully until he died; his relationship with the peregrine falcon on Mount Alverna; his invention of the Christmas crèche; the many miracles associated with Francis's life; and the role of Francis and his followers in bringing to an end Europe's Dark Ages. I hope that this book will lead children to learn more about Saint Francis and to be inspired by the lessons of his life.

Assisi, Italy

Near the beginning of the thirteenth century

LATE ONE NIGHT, the people of Assisi awoke to the sounds of boisterous laughter, music, and singing from the narrow streets of the medieval town. They shook their heads and covered their ears, yet most of them could not help smiling. Of course, the hilarious songs were the work of that charming rogue Francis Bernadone.

All Assisi knew Francis as the "King of Youth," the leader of an army of wild young men who were lavish with money and thought only of colorful costumes and crazy parties. He was a foolish rapscallion, but no one could stay mad at him for long because he was so charming and generous. Francis had black eyes and a kindly face, and he always seemed happy. His strong, musical voice could melt men's hearts. He desperately wanted to be a knight—fearless and pure of heart like King Arthur's knights of legend—or a troubadour, a traveling minstrel who composed poems and sang about love and chivalry.

Lord, make me an instrument of Your Peace

In Assisi, everyone loved Francis. He was famous for his manners and his unselfishness. He felt joy at his own good fortune and wanted to share his luck with others. As a boy, Francis vowed that he would give money to every beggar he met.

Francis's mother, Pica, taught him to love God and told him stories of the knights and their heroic deeds. She was proud of Francis for his kind heart. When Francis came home without his shoes or coat, she knew he had given them to some poor beggar. She noticed that Francis always put extra food on the family table, so that he could sneak off to share the leftovers with the poor.

Once when Francis was waiting on a wealthy customer in his father's shop, a ragged man came in to beg. Seeing that Francis was busy, the beggar left. When Francis finished selling cloth to the rich man, he locked the shop and dashed toward the marketplace, searching Assisi's steep, narrow streets until he was nearly out of breath. Finally, he found the startled beggar in the piazza and pressed into his hands the money from his last sale. Francis's father, Pietro, would have been furious if he had caught his son giving away money, clothes, and food to paupers. He was the richest cloth merchant in the city, and he loved to count his gold.

Where there is hatred, let me sow

When Francis was twenty years old, war broke out between Assisi and the nearby city of Perugia. At last he could fulfill his dream of becoming a knight. Francis was the first of his friends to join the company of soldiers who fought with long spears called lances.

Francis fought valiantly at the battle of St. John's Bridge, but he and his fellow lancers were captured and thrown into a dark dungeon in Perugia. There he always shared his food and took care of sick prisoners. His jokes and laughter lifted the spirits of the men.

After a year in prison, Francis returned home a hero, but soon afterward he fell ill. One night, in a terrible fever, Francis had a vivid dream. He saw swords and shields in the shape of a cross. He took this to mean he should become a knight and fight for God. At that time, the Pope had called for knights from all over the world to fight the enemies of the Christian church.

The next day he bought a horse, armor, and a sword and rode off to join the Pope's war against the German king, hoping for military glory. But God wanted Francis to be a different kind of knight and struck him with a sickness that made him fall from his horse on his way to battle. Then God sent Francis a vision telling him to return to Assisi to learn the true nature of his knighthood.

Francis limped home filled with sadness. For weeks he rode the surrounding countryside wondering what he should do with his life. And then one day, he saw something he feared far more than battle or death. He saw a leper.

Although Francis was as lionhearted as the bravest of knights, he feared lepers. Francis couldn't bear the sight of these lonely, miserable derelicts, with their missing fingers, ears, and noses; their bleeding sores, their scabby faces. He was disgusted by the smell of their rotting flesh. It frightened him to think that just by being near them, he might catch their disease.

Lepers were made to live in the woods far from towns and to carry bells so people could hear them approach and run for their lives. If Francis saw a leper in the distance or heard those bells, he would turn his horse and gallop away.

On this particular day, Francis came upon a leper as he rounded a bend in the road. His first instinct was to flee. Then he scolded himself for adding to the man's misery. Instead of racing away, he dismounted. Gently pressing a bag of money into the leper's hand, Francis embraced the wretched man. A great happiness flooded his whole being.

Francis's deed had taken more courage than all his reckless bravery at the battle of St. John's Bridge. He was filled with such joy that he rode to a leper colony two miles from Assisi and begged the pardon of all the lepers. He kissed each of them and gave them his clothes and his money.

where there is doubt, Faith

Francis continued to wander the countryside looking for a mission to which he could devote his life. Each day during this period of seeking, Francis would pray in San Damiano, an ancient chapel half a mile from Assisi. One day he heard a voice. *Francis, do you see that my house is in ruins? Go and restore it for me.* Francis believed that this was a message from God, telling him to rebuild the dilapidated church.

Overjoyed to have a new vocation, he went home and sold his own horse and a bale of his father's best cloth to buy stones and mortar for the task. But his greedy father did not share Francis's enthusiasm for taking orders from disembodied voices—particularly when it cost him money. In a rage, he chained his son in a dungeon and beat him savagely, demanding that Francis return the money.

When Francis refused, his father dragged him to court before Bishop Guido at the bishop's palace in the central piazza of Assisi. All the townspeople filled the piazza, eager to watch a feud between the patriarch of one of Assisi's wealthiest families and his wayward son.

where there is despair,

Bishop Guido was a wise and holy man. He admired Francis for his bravery and his love of God, but he told the boy to return his father's money. With that, Francis stripped naked and handed his father the money and his clothing. "Before this day," he announced in his strong, musical voice, "I have called Pietro Bernadone my father, but now I return his money and all the other things he has given me. Now God is my only father!"

Standing naked in front of the entire town did not help Francis's reputation. Just a few months before, the people of Assisi had considered him their hero. They had cheered as he rode out of town in glistening armor, vowing to fight for the Church and glory. When he returned a few days later, some people suspected he was a coward. Then he stole his father's cloth, and others thought him a thief. Now everyone was certain he was a lunatic. People laughed at him. Children threw mud and stones at him. He had become the biggest fool in Assisi.

Francis the fool marched naked from the piazza into the snow-covered woods. But instead of feeling sad and embarrassed, Francis was filled with joy. As the forest enveloped him, all Assisi heard him loudly singing the ballads of the troubadours.

A hermit gave Francis a tunic of rough cloth and a piece of rope for a belt. Francis dressed in this modest garb and went to live with the lepers, caring for them as he had before. When he returned to Assisi, it was as a beggar singing troubadour songs on street corners and pleading for stones instead of food. People laughed as they gave him stones and mortar, which he lugged downhill to repair the church of San Damiano. When generous folk threw him bread, he took only the hardest crusts or the stalest pieces, saving the choicer morsels for the lepers or other beggars.

Francis gave himself up to prayer, fasting, manual labor, and service with the same ferocity he had devoted to the adventures of war. He lived in the woods and called the sun and moon his brothers. He wrote beautiful poems and sang as he walked through the forests and fields. He made himself the poorest man in the world. But instead of being miserable, he became happier. "Blessed is he who expects nothing," Francis would later say, "for he will enjoy everything."

Many people thought he was crazy. But others began listening to his words.

A wealthy nobleman named Bernard was the first to announce that he would join Francis in his life of poverty and service to others. Francis suggested that they seek guidance from God. After praying, they asked the priest to let his Bible fall open three times and read whatever he saw on the page before him.

The first passage said, "Go sell what you have and give it to the poor." The priest let the Bible fall open a second time and read, "Do not keep gold or silver or money in your purse, no wallet for your journey, and only one pair of sandals and a single tunic." The third passage read: "If anyone wishes to come to me, let him deny himself and take up his cross and follow me."

That very day, the two sold all Bernard's possessions and filled a large bag with gold coins for the poor.

A greedy priest named Sylvester saw Francis and Bernard giving away great fistfuls of gold to the happy beggars of Assisi. Squeezing through the crowd he shouted, "I gave you rocks for your church, but you never paid me!"

"Here you are," said Francis, handing Sylvester several gold coins from Bernard's bag. "If you want more, just say so."

The priest went home, feeling horror at his greed. That night, Sylvester's guilt would not let him sleep. He felt the gold coins like a great weight crushing his chest. The next day, he joyfully gave his own belongings to the poor and joined Francis and Bernard in the woods.

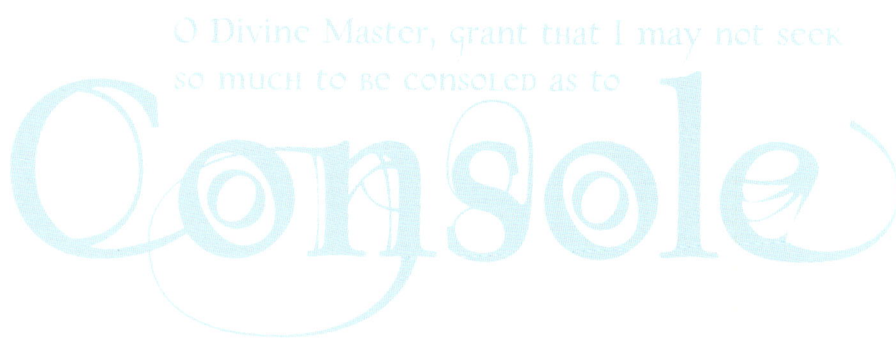

Within a few months, several men had joined Francis, including knights, priests, noblemen, a troubadour, a farmer, and a judge.

These men called each other "friar," meaning *brother,* and lived in simple huts made of branches and mud. They worked in monasteries or on farms, caring for lepers and giving all the money they earned each day to the poor, trusting in God to provide for tomorrow. They tried to live like Christ and His apostles, to carry nothing, and to find great joy in mingling with the sick, beggars, and other wretches. When they numbered twelve "brothers," they traveled to Rome to receive a blessing from the Pope.

As word spread about the friars, noble and courageous men in droves sold their belongings and followed Francis in poverty. Soon thousands of brothers were wandering all over Europe, serenading passersby with songs of joy. They ate roots and berries, performed good deeds, and comforted the sick. They could be seen on all the roads in Italy, Sweden, France, and Spain, walking two by two.

Just as King Arthur's knights had met once a year at the Round Table to share stories of their adventures, the friars would gather every few years in the forests and fields surrounding a woodland church that Francis had rebuilt from ruins, called the Portiuncula. There they rejoiced in God and prayed and ate together before scattering again across the land. Francis taught them that the Gospel, like the code of chivalry, required that they rejoice even when they were suffering, and that they should never complain and never blame anyone.

Happiness does not come from comfort or material possessions, Francis said, but from serving others. Francis reminded his friars that they should give to every beggar who asked. "If a thief steals your socks," he would tell them, "you should run after him and give him your shoes."

to be understood as to

Francis's example also inspired many women. One of these was Clare, a beautiful girl from a noble Assisi family. Her parents wanted her to marry, but she had a great yearning to give her life to the poor. She felt that her soul had been set on fire by the poetry of Francis's sermons.

When she was fifteen, she crept through a hole in the stone wall of her parents' castle garden with her cousin Pacificci, who also wanted to give her life to God and the poor. Friars with torches met the young women in the woods, where Francis cut off their hair before the altar of the Holy Angels and gave them rough tunics like his own. Then he led the girls to the monastery of the Benedictine nuns, two miles away.

Many of Clare's family members traveled to the monastery and vainly tried to persuade the girls to return. When Clare's younger sister Agnes made her own escape a week later, their fierce uncle Monaldo stormed the monastery with a dozen knights to capture the girls and bring them home. One horseman dragged poor Agnes by her hair over sharp stones down the rugged mountain path. "Help me, sister!" Agnes shouted to Clare. When Clare heard her pleas, she fell to her knees and prayed to God for help. Suddenly Agnes became so heavy that none of the men could move her even one inch more.

Although Clare was young, she inspired thousands of women to give up their worldly possessions and join in the life of poverty and service to others. This order of sisters became known as the Poor Clares. A great leader and a clever speaker, Clare could even persuade kings and princes to do her bidding on behalf of the poor.

In Clare, Francis had found a friend for life. Although they met rarely, they cared for each other and shared a deep love of God and nature.

Francis loved animals and plants, the sea and the stars, and the beauty of the world that God gave us. He thought of God as a great artist who was best known through His creations. Francis believed that destroying any living creature was a sin against God and humanity, who benefitted from the joy and wonder that each creature inspired. He called all his fellow creatures "sister" and "brother."

He forbade friars to chop down living trees, and he would pick worms off the firewood to keep them from being burned. In the winter he brought warm wine and honey to the wild bees. Once he traded his cloak for two lambs that were being hauled to the butcher and allowed them to live out their lives at the Portiuncula. One of these devoted sheep followed Francis everywhere. It would kneel during Mass and always bleated respectfully when passing a statue of the Holy Virgin.

One day Francis said to his companions, "Stay by the road and wait for me while I preach to our sisters the birds." Francis walked to a nearby meadow, and as soon as he began his sermon, birds from every direction gathered around him to listen. They sat in silence even when his tunic brushed against them as he walked back and forth. When he finished, the birds showed their great joy by singing and spreading their wings.

Francis's life was filled with similar incidents. At Greccio, a hare followed Francis like a dog. When he was at Lake Rieti, a kingfisher and the fishes came each day to hear him preach, and a knight gave him a pheasant that stayed with him until he died. In the spring and summer evenings at the Portiuncula, a cicada would land in his hand when he called and sang with him.

For it is in giving that we Receive

Even fierce animals loved Francis, including the most ferocious of all, the wolf of Gubbio.

Once Francis visited the town of Gubbio, where the people could talk of nothing but a wolf of extraordinary size and appetite that was devouring their animals, as well as some men, women, and children.

Francis wanted to talk to this wicked wolf. Everyone begged him not to, but when Francis insisted, the people climbed atop the city walls for a better view. No one had ever seen a saint eaten by a wolf. (Even then, many people considered him a saint.) Men trembled and women screamed in terror when they saw the snarling animal charge Francis from the woods, its ravenous jaws wide, its teeth flashing.

But Francis made the sign of the cross, and the wolf came to a sudden stop. "Come here, Brother Wolf," Francis said. "In Christ's name, I forbid you to be wicked." Hearing this, the wolf dropped his head and lay at Francis's feet.

Francis scolded the wolf for its dreadful crimes and ordered it to stop eating the villagers and their animals. He promised to tell the people of Gubbio to not harm the wolf.

Miraculously, the wolf obeyed. For the rest of its life, the wolf lived peacefully in Gubbio—fed, cared for, and loved by the townspeople, because it reminded them of Francis's visit.

Francis had lived a happy life serving others, acting as guardian to God's creatures, performing miracles, and inspiring men and women to devote themselves to poverty. Now Francis knew that his end was near, and he traveled the countryside on his donkey, urging crowds to love their fellow creatures. He was blind and suffered excruciating headaches and other illnesses and could rarely eat. Yet he was more cheerful than ever. Knowing that he would soon be in paradise with Jesus, his torments became a delight. It was at this time that he wrote his famous song "Canticle of the Sun," which praises the natural world that God created for our enrichment and enjoyment.

On his final day, Francis had himself taken from his hut and placed naked on the cold ground as a symbol of his life's work. Since the day when he had stood naked in front of all Assisi and given his life to God, he had not accumulated a single material object. He was returning to his God as he had entered the world.

As twilight enveloped the land, Francis saw his visitor coming. "Welcome, Sister Death!" he said joyfully. "It is you who will introduce me to eternal life."

Then, looking up, Francis saw God in all His glory. The stars that night, as they rose, gazed down upon the happiest man who had ever lived. At the instant of his death, a multitude of Francis's beloved larks descended on his hut and sang songs of great exultation.

All night the woods rang with the singing of the birds and of the friars who had camped there by the hundreds to bid Francis good-bye. Together they celebrated their great knight, whose life had been a love poem to God and Creation.

That evening, the earth and all its creatures had lost their greatest friend.

Time Line

1182 Francis is born in Assisi and christened "Giovanni" (John). His father renames him "Francesco" (Francis), meaning "Frenchman."

1202 Francis fights valiantly but is captured with his fellow lancers during the battle of St. John's Bridge on the Tiber River, below Perugia.

1203 Francis is released a year later, and becomes a popular hero in Assisi.

1204 Francis equips himself as a knight and rides off to join the army of Pope Innocent III, in the Fourth Crusade. Sudden illness befalls him on the road to battle. In Francis's feverish vision, God instructs him to return to Assisi for another kind of knighthood.

1206 In the chapel of San Damiano, Francis hears a voice directing him to "repair my house which is falling in ruins." Although Francis humbly takes this direction to mean he should rebuild the ruined chapel at San Damiano, most Christians today commonly accept that he was called to become an example for the whole Catholic Church, which had become wealthy and corrupt. After Francis sells his father's cloth to help pay for San Damiano's restoration, his father has him dragged into court. Stripping himself of his worldly possessions, Francis enters the forest and commits his life to God.

1208 The first followers of Francis repent their sins and join him in the forest.

1209 Francis visits Rome with his twelve friars. Pope Innocent at first refuses to speak to the peculiar beggar. However, after dreaming that the ragged derelict, to whom he had earlier denied an audience, was holding up a toppling church, the Pope summons Francis and approves the friars' simple order embracing poverty.

1212 On Palm Sunday, Clare Scifi escapes her home and takes the vows of sisterhood before Francis. Francis makes his first attempt to visit Crusaders in the Holy Land. His ship is blown off course and he is stranded on the Dalmatian coast.

1213 Francis delivers his sermon to the birds near Cannara.

1214 Francis meets and kisses Saint Dominic at the Lateran in Rome. Their friendship inspires centuries of warm relations between Franciscans and Dominicans. At an annual "Chapter of the Mats," around the Portiuncula, 5,000 friars gather, and Francis calls volunteers to do their good works beyond the Italian border.

1218 By now friars are a common sight all over Italy, southern France, and Spain.

1219 Francis goes to the Holy Land and preaches first to the Crusaders and then to the sultan Al Malik Al Kamil, who offers him rich presents and begs him to remain in his court. When Francis refuses, the sultan gives him safe conduct through Muslim lands.

1221 Anthony of Padua joins the order, inspired by the deaths of five martyred friars in Morocco. Francis launches the "third order," opening the opportunity for lay and married people to commit themselves to Franciscan principles. Among the tens of thousands who joined over the following decades are Dante, Petrarch, Raphael, Michelangelo, Christopher Columbus, and other great thinkers who help revitalize the church and bring an end to the Dark Ages.

1223 Francis invents the first Christian crèche in a mountain cave near Greccio, where he celebrates Christmas Mass with hundreds of townspeople before a manger with cows and donkeys and sheep.

1224 Francis receives the stigmata on the summit of Mount Alverna.

1225 Francis writes "Canticle of the Sun," reciting it the first time for Sister Clare.

1226 Francis dies at the Portiuncula.

1228 Francis is canonized by Pope Gregory IX in Assisi.

The feast day of Saint Francis is celebrated on October 4 and the feast of Saint Clare on August 11.

JOSHUA LAWRENCE CHAMBERLAIN

AMERICAN HERO

ROBERT F. KENNEDY, JR.

Illustrated by Nikita Andreev

Sky Pony Press
New York, NY

ACKNOWLEDGMENTS

My son Conor inspired me to write this book when he undertook a writing project on Joshua Chamberlain for his fifth grade history class at Brunswick School. Conor acted as my researcher, providing me with answers to every question I asked about Chamberlain and the various battles of the Civil War. I also want to gratefully acknowledge my friend Val Chamberlain, who provided a number of research articles for this book.

Box Set Edition 2026

Sky Pony Press books may be purchased in bulk at special discounts for sales promotion, corporate gifts, fund-raising, or educational purposes. Special editions can also be created to specifications. For details, contact the Special Sales Department, Sky Pony Press, 307 Fifth Avenue, 4th Floor, New York, NY 10016 or info@skyhorsepublishing.com.

Sky Pony® is a registered trademark of Skyhorse Publishing, Inc.®, a Delaware corporation.

Visit our website at www.skyponypress.com.
Please follow our publisher Tony Lyons on Instagram @tonylyonsisuncertain

10 9 8 7 6 5 4 3 2 1

Library of Congress Cataloging-in-Publication Data is available on file.

Cover design by Kai Texel

Map of Gettysburg on page iv © Bettman/Corbis
Photograph on page vi © Corbis
Photograph on page viii by Jacques Lowe
Photograph on page 37 courtesy of Maine Historical Society

Sources for asterisked quotes are listed on page 38.

Print ISBN: 978-1-5107-8682-0
Ebook ISBN: 978-1-5107-7957-0

Manufactured in China, January 2026
This product conforms to CPSIA 2008

To the courageous men and women of America's armed forces

—R.F.K., Jr.

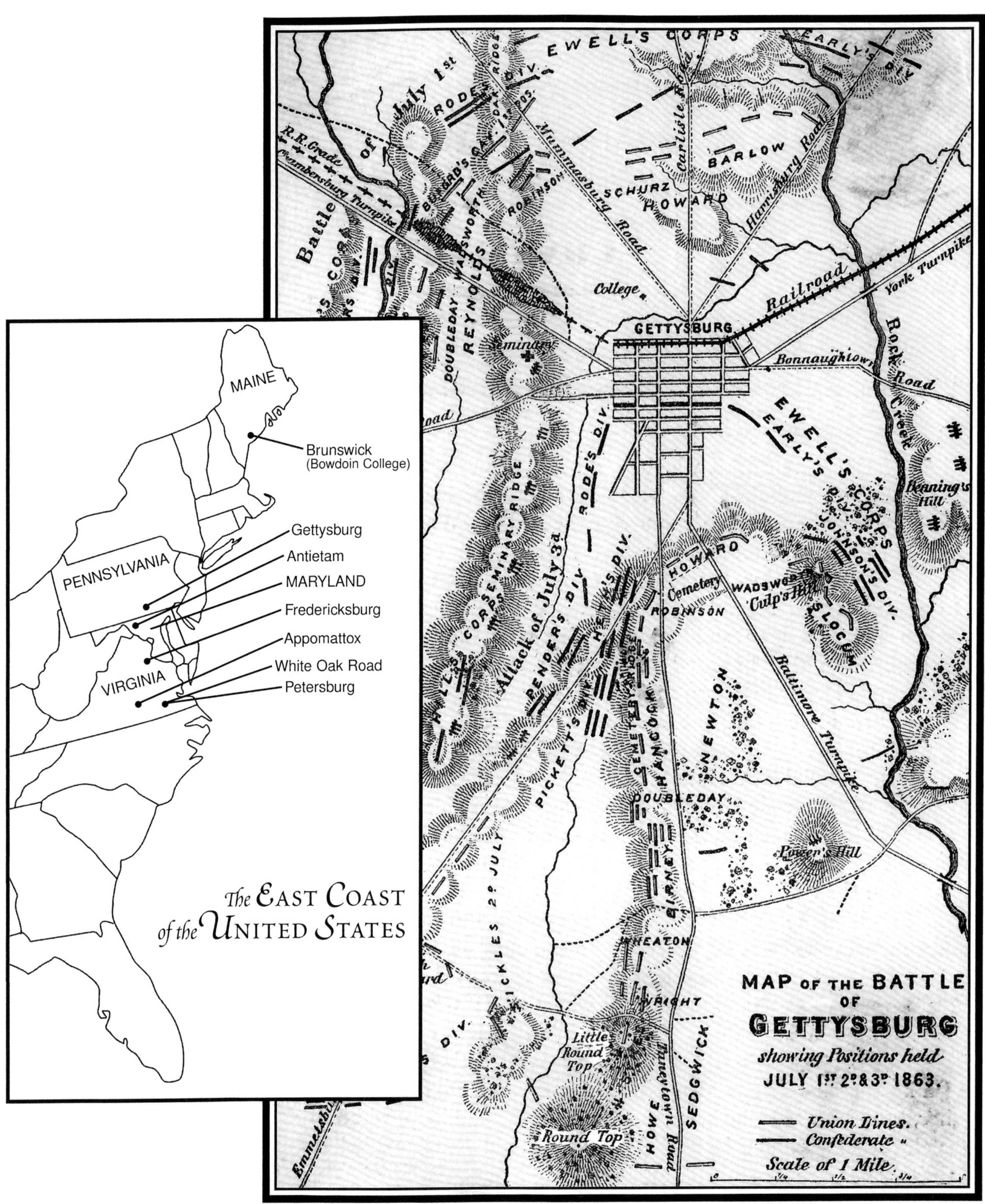

MAP OF THE BATTLE OF GETTYSBURG
showing Positions held
JULY 1st 2d & 3d 1863.
Union Lines.
Confederate "
Scale of 1 Mile
GETTYSBURG
EWELL'S CORPS
EARLY'S DIV.
RODES DIV.
Battle of July 1st
R.R. Grade
Chambersburg Turnpike
Mummasburg Road
Carlisle Road
Harrisburg Road
BARLOW
SCHURZ
HOWARD
ROBINSON
WADSWORTH
DOUBLEDAY
REYNOLDS
College
Railroad
York Turnpike
Seminary
Bonnaughtown Road
Rock Creek
Benning's Hill
EARLY'S
RODES'S DIV.
SEMINARY RIDGE
Attack of July 3d
PENDER'S DIV.
HETH'S DIV.
PICKETT'S DIV.
HILL'S CORPS
Cemetery
Culp's Hill
JOHNSON'S DIV.
SLOCUM
Baltimore Turnpike
NEWTON
CEMETERY RIDGE
HANCOCK
DOUBLEDAY
BIRNEY
Power's Hill
SICKLES 2d JULY
WHEATON
WRIGHT
Little Round Top
Round Top
HOWE
SEDGWICK
Taneytown Road
Emmetsburg
MAINE
Brunswick
(Bowdoin College)
Gettysburg
Antietam
MARYLAND
Fredericksburg
Appomattox
White Oak Road
Petersburg
PENNSYLVANIA
VIRGINIA
The East Coast of the United States

CONTENTS

Foreword/vii

1 "Just Do It!"/1

2 Lieutenant Colonel Chamberlain/5

3 Fredericksburg/8

4 Gettysburg/11

5 Little Round Top/12

6 Big Round Top/20

7 Petersburg/23

8 Victory at White Oak Road/27

9 Appomattox/33

Quotation Sources/38

Bibliography/38

Suggested Reading/38

Joshua Chamberlain, circa 1864

FOREWORD

Sometimes the fate of a nation rests upon the shoulders of a single courageous soul.

ONE DAY IN JULY 1863, a young college professor named Joshua Chamberlain and a handful of gallant boys from Maine risked—and in some cases, gave—their lives to hold a few acres of rough, rocky soil on a Pennsylvania hilltop. Their heroic deeds saved our country from destruction. Their legacy is the United States of America, and the courage, character, and goodness that make our country a great nation.

Had Chamberlain or his men faltered, even momentarily, during the fight for the Round Tops, our nation would have died at Gettysburg. After that battle, Chamberlain and the men of the 20th Maine buried their dead, side by side, in a single long grave. They memorialized each of their fallen comrades with a plank torn from an ammunition box and inscribed with the soldier's name. As he completed this grim task, Chamberlain wistfully hoped that generations of Americans who "know us not" would come from afar, "to see where and by whom great things were suffered and done for them."

I wrote this book in the hope that our children will put a higher value on America and its freedoms if they understand the high price at which these things were purchased by an earlier generation of our countrymen. The recitation of a glorious history and heroic deeds has the power to imbue us with noble thoughts and summons us to the ideals and courage that make America great.

The author as a child with his father

In their efforts to improve our minds and elevate our souls, my parents encouraged their eleven children to read history and learn about the great heroes of the past. My father, an avid military historian, told us, over dinner, the stories of important battles like Bunker Hill, the Cowpens, and Bull Run. Our family visited the decisive battlefields of the Revolution and the Civil War. On one of these trips, to Gettysburg, we heard the story of the citizen soldier Joshua Chamberlain.

Chamberlain epitomized the best qualities of the American character. He was a hardworking farmer; a poet and a musician; a linguist, writer, and theologian. He was educated and idealistic. He was self-reliant, kind, fair, and decent. He had character, integrity, and manners. He loved America and was willing to sacrifice his life and fortune for our country. His astounding feats of daring in the nation's time of greatest peril compare with epic deeds of the warriors of ancient times and legend.

The extraordinary thing is how common these virtues were in so many of those who fought in the Civil War, on both sides. Indeed, the Civil War is the story of millions of acts of heartbreaking gallantry. Chamberlain and his contemporaries faced crises far more dire than any known to this generation. More than 620,000 American soldiers died in that conflict, a catastrophe equivalent to the loss of 5.7 million Americans relative to the country's population today. Our nation faced imminent destruction. Whole cities were besieged and ruined; our countryside was immolated; railroads and roads destroyed. Yet, the Americans fighting for the Union cause did not compromise their principles or their commitment to justice. They never dismissed their vision of a noble and just America as if it were a luxury that we could no longer afford. Their dauntlessness transformed the Civil War from America's gravest and most tragic episode into our country's finest hour. Its successful prosecution required great national sacrifice, the guidance of Providence, and extraordinary heroics by thousands of citizens, from President Lincoln to the lowest infantryman. Their efforts saved the Union and abolished slavery, which had torn the moral fiber of our young republic. They helped confirm America as the generous, principled nation we became in our own eyes—and in the eyes of the world. When he spoke of the war, Chamberlain referred to it, in the common parlance of the day, as "the noble cause." Chamberlain and his soldiers fought the war to preserve not just the solidarity but the virtues of our nation—our idealism, faith, optimism, decency, and commitment to justice. The most conspicuous quality of these men was courage.

In the view of earlier American generations, courage was practically synonymous with freedom; fear, after all, was the instrument of tyrants. As Franklin Roosevelt later put it, the greatest enemy of our treasured freedom is "fear itself." Every once in a while, we Americans need to remind ourselves that we are the land of the free precisely *because* we are the home of the brave! A nation of great ideals can be preserved only by sacrifice and courage. I grew up thinking of Americans as the bravest people on earth. Americans, our civics instructors taught us, were guided by principle and willing to sacrifice all to preserve our rights and liberty.

It is the fantastic bravery of a long line of stalwarts like Joshua Chamberlain, and their love of principle, their commitment to ideals, and their willingness to sacrifice, which has defined our people and guided our nation's destiny. It's worth considering today how grievously we would dishonor the memory of these gallant heroes if we should ever let America become a nation governed by fear, or if we willingly compromised the rights they gave so much to guarantee.

—Robert F. Kennedy, Jr.

1.

"JUST DO IT!"

Joshua Chamberlain was born September 8, 1828, in Brewer, Maine, the oldest of five children. His parents required their children to be honest, honorable, and cheerful. Joshua had to practice good manners and the knightly traits of humor, courtesy, and generosity. Joshua worked hard on his family farm and grew up to be slim and muscular, handsome and tall, with piercing blue eyes. He learned to ride, to sail, and to fence with swords. He was a crack shot, but he hated killing animals. He loved poetry and played the piano and violin. Joshua eventually learned ten languages, including the language of the Aroostook Indians, who lived in birch-bark wigwams on his family's hundred-acre farm.

When he was thirteen, Joshua got the axle of a hay wagon stuck between two large rocks on his father's farm. With 400 pounds of hay on the wagon, the oxen could go neither forward nor back. Joshua's father ordered him to free the wagon and get it moving. When Joshua

asked, "How should I do it, Father?" his dad replied angrily, "Just do it!" With an act of superhuman strength that he didn't know he had, the young boy lifted the wagon, and the oxen started off with a jerk. No one was more surprised than Joshua, and the lesson stayed with him for life. From that day on, he had a sense that even the worst obstacles could be overcome with effort. A big problem he faced as a boy was an embarrassing stutter. But he worked hard to overcome it and eventually became a superb public speaker and even a professor of rhetoric!

Joshua's mother wanted him to be a minister, and his father hoped he would make a career in the army as had his grandfathers, both of whom had fought in the American Revolution. But Joshua felt trapped by all the rules and "petty despotisms" of both the ministry and the military. He loved ideas and the freedom to think and read, so he won a position as a professor at Bowdoin College, where he taught French, German, Greek, Latin, and Rhetoric. He married Fannie Adams, and the couple settled into a quiet college routine and eventually produced five children.

Joshua loved this life. But then Abraham Lincoln was elected president of the United States and threatened to abolish slavery. The slave states declared war and tried to split our country in two. Joshua hated slavery, which he would later call "a pox on the nation." And he loved America. When the Civil War began, Joshua knew he could not stay out of the fray. He wrote, "But, I fear, this war, so costly of blood and treasure, will not cease until the men of the North are willing to leave good positions, and sacrifice the dearest personal interests, to rescue our Country from desolation. . . . every man ought to come forward and ask to be placed at his proper post."* He left his family and Bowdoin College to volunteer for the Union army in 1862. He was thirty-four years old.

2.
LIEUTENANT COLONEL CHAMBERLAIN

ALTHOUGH HE LACKED ANY MILITARY BACKGROUND, Joshua's strong education landed him the rank of lieutenant colonel in the newly formed 20th Maine Infantry Regiment. He worked hard to make himself a good leader. He read every manual and military history he could find and studied books about maneuvers and tactics by lantern in his tent, late into the night. Each day he drilled his men tirelessly, a routine that would save their lives and our nation at Gettysburg. "It is the discipline which is the soul of armies," he later said. "Other things—moral considerations, impulses of sentiment, and even natural excitement—may lead men to great deeds; but taken in the long run, and in all vicissitudes, an army is effective in proportion to its discipline."*

Joshua's men despised the constant drilling but idolized their lieutenant. Although officers were entitled to better food and conditions, Joshua cheerfully underwent the same hardships as his men. He slept

outdoors, using his saddle as a pillow and wrapping himself in a rubber blanket when it rained. When he ordered his men to do chores, such as building fortifications, he would strip off his shirt, pick up a shovel or ax, and work side by side with them.

3.
FREDERICKSBURG

JOSHUA'S REGIMENT LEFT MAINE, bound for Washington, where it joined the Union army. Joshua's first battle was the bloodiest day in American history. General Robert E. Lee's Confederate army had invaded the Union state of Maryland and was caught at Antietam on September 17, 1862. Joshua and his regiment, held in reserve, watched the terrible slaughter from the sidelines. More than 22,700 Americans, on both sides, were killed or wounded. The Union army suffered the most casualties, but General Lee was driven back into the South.

The Union army chased the Confederates across the Potomac River, catching them at Fredericksburg, Virginia. There, on December 13, 1862, the wily General Lee turned and dealt the bluecoats a terrible defeat. The 20th Maine was in the forefront of the battle.

More than 78,000 Confederates occupied the frozen high ground behind a stone wall near Fredericksburg. They were besieged by 115,000 Union troops. Because of a bungled battle plan, fourteen

Yankee regiments charged the Rebs, one at a time, and were mowed down. Not a single bluecoat ever reached the Confederate trenches. Joshua's horse was shot as he rode into the battle, and he was thrown into the Potomac. He was unharmed, but he and his men were trapped on the plain west of the city, where they fought all night behind a breastwork of bodies of their fallen comrades. Joshua was wounded when a musket ball grazed his neck and right ear. The next morning, the Union generals, seeing the hopelessness of their position, ordered their battered army to withdraw.

4.
GETTYSBURG

EMBOLDENED BY THIS VICTORY, General Lee again invaded the North the following summer, in 1863. General Lee wanted to capture a Northern city, such as Washington or Baltimore, and then force President Lincoln to sign a peace treaty allowing the Confederacy to secede. After marching for two days in crushing heat, mostly without food or sleep, the Union army caught Lee near a Pennsylvania village named Gettysburg.

Joshua's 20th Maine had only 238 of the 500 men that would comprise a full regiment. As the army assembled at Gettysburg, General George Gordon Meade delivered to him, at gunpoint, 120 mutineers from a disbanded Maine unit with orders that Joshua "make them do their duty or shoot them down."

After questioning the deserters, Joshua concluded they'd been badly mistreated. He promised to plead their case with the generals, and told them that if they followed him, he would treat them as soldiers should be treated. Inspired by his leadership and fairness, they turned out to be among his best fighters.

5.
LITTLE ROUND TOP

EVEN AS THE UNION ARMY WAS ARRIVING AT GETTYSBURG, the Confederates launched their attack. Little did Joshua know that this day the fate of his nation rested on his shoulders. Joshua's corps commander, Colonel Strong Vincent, pointed to a hill named Little Round Top that overlooked Cemetery Ridge, where the Union army was digging in to make its stand. If the Confederate army took that hill, it could rain down artillery that would quickly destroy the Union forces. General Lee would then be able to conquer Washington, Baltimore, and Philadelphia. The South could win the Civil War. The Confederates had already swept over the neighboring hill, Big Round Top, and they were racing to occupy Little Round Top. Colonel Vincent ordered Joshua to "hold that ground at all hazards."

Joshua raced up Little Round Top on horseback beside his two brothers, Tom and John. Both brothers had followed Joshua's example and joined the Union cause. Tom was one of Joshua's twenty-eight junior officers, and John was serving as an army chaplain. As they rode, a Confederate cannonball missed them by only inches. Joshua ordered his brothers to separate. "Another such shot," he told them, "might make it a hard day for Mother."

Joshua narrowly beat the Confederates to the summit of Little Round Top. But before his men had the chance to dig in, the Confederates mounted a hot attack, hoping to capture the hill. As Joshua's soldiers took their positions, they were already being bombarded by cannons and picked off by sharpshooters. Rebel shells came screaming down upon them. A splinter of shrapnel tore through Joshua's boot, slicing his foot. When the Confederate cannonading finally stopped, there was an ominous silence, and Joshua knew the charge was coming.

Joshua had faith in his Maine men. Each of them understood the consequences of losing this hill to the Confederates. He saw the bravery and determination in their faces. His men knew that Joshua's calmness masked a heart of steel and the soul of a great warrior.

Then the terrifying howl of the Rebel yell rose above the roar of musket fire and electrified the air. The Confederate army fell heavily on the 20th Maine's entire line. Their first charge took the Rebels to ten feet from Joshua before a terrible hail of bullets from the 20th

Maine beat them back. The Confederates caught their breath, regrouped, and charged once more, battering Joshua's lines again and again with waves of desperate assaults. Sometimes they would drive Joshua's boys back a few yards, but each time, the 20th Maine would fight ferociously and regain the lost ground. For two full hours, the edge of the fight rolled backward and forward like a wave. To Joshua there seemed to be no end to the attacks. But he walked calmly up and down the line, giving his soldiers words of encouragement. Often, at great risk, he ventured out in front of his men to read the battlefield.

From this vantage, he spotted Confederate Colonel William Oates's Alabama regiment climbing stealthily around the hill through the underbrush to flank him on the left and attack his line from the rear. His long study of military history and tactics allowed him to quickly devise a plan to meet this attack. He ordered his troops to keep up rapid fire while sidestepping to the left between shots, extending his left line in a horseshoe to open up a new front at his rear. The constant drilling paid off. His men executed the complicated maneuver on the rough hillside terrain with energy, quickness, and precision that made even Joshua marvel. In a few minutes, the Confederates charged from their hiding places in the bushes with a bloodcurdling howl and rifles firing. But instead of meeting the undefended rear of Joshua's line, the Rebels encountered musket fire from Joshua's boys that tore their charge to pieces. Colonel Oates was shocked at the power of the Union defense, which he later described as "the most destructive fire I had ever seen."

Now greycoats were flooding the hill on all sides with fury. Through the gun smoke, Joshua saw the powder-blackened faces of his troops as they wrestled with Confederates in savage hand-to-hand fighting, cutting, thrusting, grappling, and firing their weapons at close range. Joshua saw "things that cannot be told or dreamed. All around, a strange mingled roar," he wrote, recalling the scene, "shouts of defiance, rally, and desperation; and underneath, murmured entreaty and stifled moans; gasping prayers, snatches of Sabbath song, whispers of loved names; everywhere men torn and broken, staggering, creeping, quivering on the earth, and dead faces with strangely fixed eyes staring stark into the sky. How men held on, each one knows—not I."* Sometimes there were more of the enemy around him than his own men. A decimating volley from the Confederate line knocked Joshua to the ground with a shot to his thigh. Fortunately, his metal sword scabbard diverted the bullet, and he rose again with a painful bruise.

But now he saw that the volley had cut a wide hole in the center of his line. Through the smoke, Joshua glimpsed the twenty-five-year-old color guard sergeant Andrew Tucker standing alone in the gaping breach, the flag braced against his shoulder. With his free hand, Tucker picked up a rifle from a fallen friend and began firing upon the graycoats who were charging him. Joshua ordered his brother Tom into the gap, knowing he might die there. When the smoke cleared, both boys were still standing, and the Rebels had withdrawn. During this short lull, Joshua ordered his soldiers to throw up a stone wall to protect themselves from the next assault. Their ammunition was nearly exhausted,

US

and the Maine soldiers scurried to gather the last remaining cartridges from their dead and wounded comrades.

Each Confederate attack seemed more intense than the last. During one assault, a Rebel sniper hiding behind a large boulder got Joshua clearly in his gun sights. Joshua's shoulder straps identified him as a lieutenant colonel, and the Rebel knew a Yankee officer would be a great trophy. Yet, when he squeezed his trigger, a strange feeling made him stop. Angry at himself for hesitating, he tried to pull the trigger again. Again he was unable to fire the deadly bullet, and he gave up. Joshua would not know till years afterward how narrowly he had escaped death.

As the beleaguered Maine soldiers divvied up their tiny store of bullets, the brave Confederates mounted their most ferocious assault of the day. With a final volley of concentrated fire, the 20th Maine drove the exhausted Rebels backward and down the hill. But now Joshua's boys were completely out of ammunition. Standing behind his thinning ranks, Joshua looked around. He watched the Confederates regather among the boulders and bushes for yet another attack. Joshua could see the effect of the repeated Confederate charges on his position. The situation looked grim. Half his men were dead or badly wounded. Some officers shouted that their units had been annihilated. The enemy forces outnumbered his by two to one. Without ammo, the shredded remains of his regiment had no hope of repulsing another attack. Colonel Strong Vincent, his commander, lay dying from a mortal wound far down the Union line on Cemetery Ridge. Joshua remembered Vincent's words: "Hold that ground at all hazards!" His desperate men looked back at him for orders. He would later remember that moment. *"My thoughts were running deep."* Suddenly, the solution occurred to him: since he was too weak to defend, he would attack!

He shouted the astounding command to "Fix bayonets!" The order flew from man to man down the line, along with the metal clash of bayonets being attached to empty rifles. Then a wild shout rose spontaneously from Joshua's desperate soldiers, and before he had a chance to shout "Charge," they were piling over the barricades and sprinting downhill toward the astonished Confederates. Brave as the Rebels were, the unexpected sight of 200 careening wild men thundering down upon them with blades of cold steel caused their courage to falter. Joshua's boys slammed into the Confederate lines with unstoppable momentum from their downhill charge, and the exhausted Confederates broke and flew in every direction or turned to raise their hands in surrender. Within minutes, Chamberlain's 200 men had taken 400 captives. Entire companies surrendered as one.

Dashing forward with his men, Joshua ran headfirst into a Confederate officer, who pointed a large navy revolver at Joshua's face and fired. Miraculously, the bullet only grazed Joshua's head. Joshua put his saber to the man's throat, and the greycoat immediately raised his hands in surrender. As Joshua took the officer's pistol, he was feeling exalted: the 20th Maine's downhill charge had broken the Rebel flank and ended the threat to Little Round Top.

6.
BIG ROUND TOP

FOLLOWING THEIR VICTORIOUS CHARGE, Joshua's men collapsed in exhaustion. But the battered survivors of the 20th Maine would neither celebrate nor sleep that night.

As twilight descended, the new corps commander, Colonel Rice, appeared at the 20th Maine's campfire. Rice, who had replaced Joshua's mortally wounded commander, Strong Vincent, had ordered another regiment to capture a neighboring hill known as Big Round Top, but its officer had refused. Frustrated, Colonel Rice was requesting—but not ordering—Joshua to perform the task. Joshua did not have the heart to command his exhausted troops into yet another fray. He told his boys, "I am going. As many of you men who feel able to do so can follow me." Then he turned, and with drawn sword, began limping up the hill on his wounded legs. Every man in the 20th Maine grabbed his musket to follow their colonel. Joshua ordered them to fix bayonets and creep quietly in the darkness. He feared that making noise would

reveal their small number to their enemy. Their stealth paid off. They surprised and captured a scouting party of twenty-five Rebels, along with a Confederate general. Baffled by the disappearance of their scouting party, the Confederate troops on Big Round Top assumed they were being surrounded by a much larger force, and fled downhill. By morning, Joshua had captured and fortified Big Round Top and received reinforcements so that it was firmly in Union control.

The Round Tops were the key to the whole battlefield at Gettysburg. The Confederates' failure to capture and keep them forced General Lee to make a full frontal attack on the center of the Union line the next day. Following Lee's orders, General George Pickett led approximately 15,000 gallant Confederates in a courageous but futile charge against Cemetery Ridge. Ten thousand graycoats died or were wounded. Pickett's Charge was the deadliest in the history of the American military. There were 51,000 casualties during the three days at Gettysburg—about as many Americans who were killed in action during the entire Vietnam war. That defeat put Lee into retreat and sapped the strength and spirit from the Confederate cause. Though the war would not officially end for two torturous years, Gettysburg was the beginning of the end for the Southern army, and Joshua Chamberlain's 20th Maine had set the stage for the Union victory.

7.
PETERSBURG

After its defeat at Gettysburg, the battered Confederate army escaped across the Potomac into the South. President Lincoln ordered General Ulysses S. Grant and his subordinate General George Meade to chase and destroy the Confederates. During the next year, Grant met Lee at many great battles across Virginia, including the Battle of the Wilderness in May, 1864, and the battles of Spotsylvania Court House and Cold Harbor later that month. In each battle, Joshua and his men fought bravely and often played important roles. Finally, the Confederate army holed up in the city of Petersburg, from which they could guard the road and rail lines to the capital of the Confederacy at Richmond. They erected strong fortifications and awaited attack.

Joshua stayed in touch with his family from the battlefield, writing long letters and short notes to Fannie and his children at every opportunity. "Dear Daisy, Do you and Wyllys have a pleasant time now-a-days? . . . How I should enjoy a May-walk with you and Wyllys, and what beautiful flowers we would bring home to surprise Mamma and Aunty! . . . I am suddenly ordered to go to the front to take command of our pickets. Mamma will tell you what they are, so goodbye once more . . . Papa."*

On June 18, 1864, General Meade ordered Joshua to lead the entire Union army in a frontal assault against the heavily fortified city down a valley called Rives' Salient. Surveying the landscape, Joshua had serious doubts about the planned attack. It meant charging across a long, open, marshy field, crossing a stream, and climbing uphill without cover, all within range of enemy guns. Joshua regarded the assignment a death sentence and asked Meade to reconsider. When Meade refused, Joshua grimly prepared to lead the attack.

Joshua drew his sword, ordered his men to charge, and began the desperate dash toward 7,500 Confederate muskets that bristled over tall Rebel fortifications mounted with powerful cannons.

The earth shook with the roar of guns, the din of shots, the screaming of horses and men. Exploding shells furrowed the ground. As Joshua climbed from the creek, ahead of the army, he was shot through by a minié ball. The bullet entered his right thigh and came out his left hip, crushing his pelvis bone and piercing his bladder and spleen. Not wanting his men to see him fall, he leaned on his sword with desperate valor and remained standing until the first wave of the charge moved past him. Then he collapsed. Joshua believed himself to be dying, so when an ambulance crew came with a stretcher to retrieve him, he ordered them to leave him where he lay and tend to the other

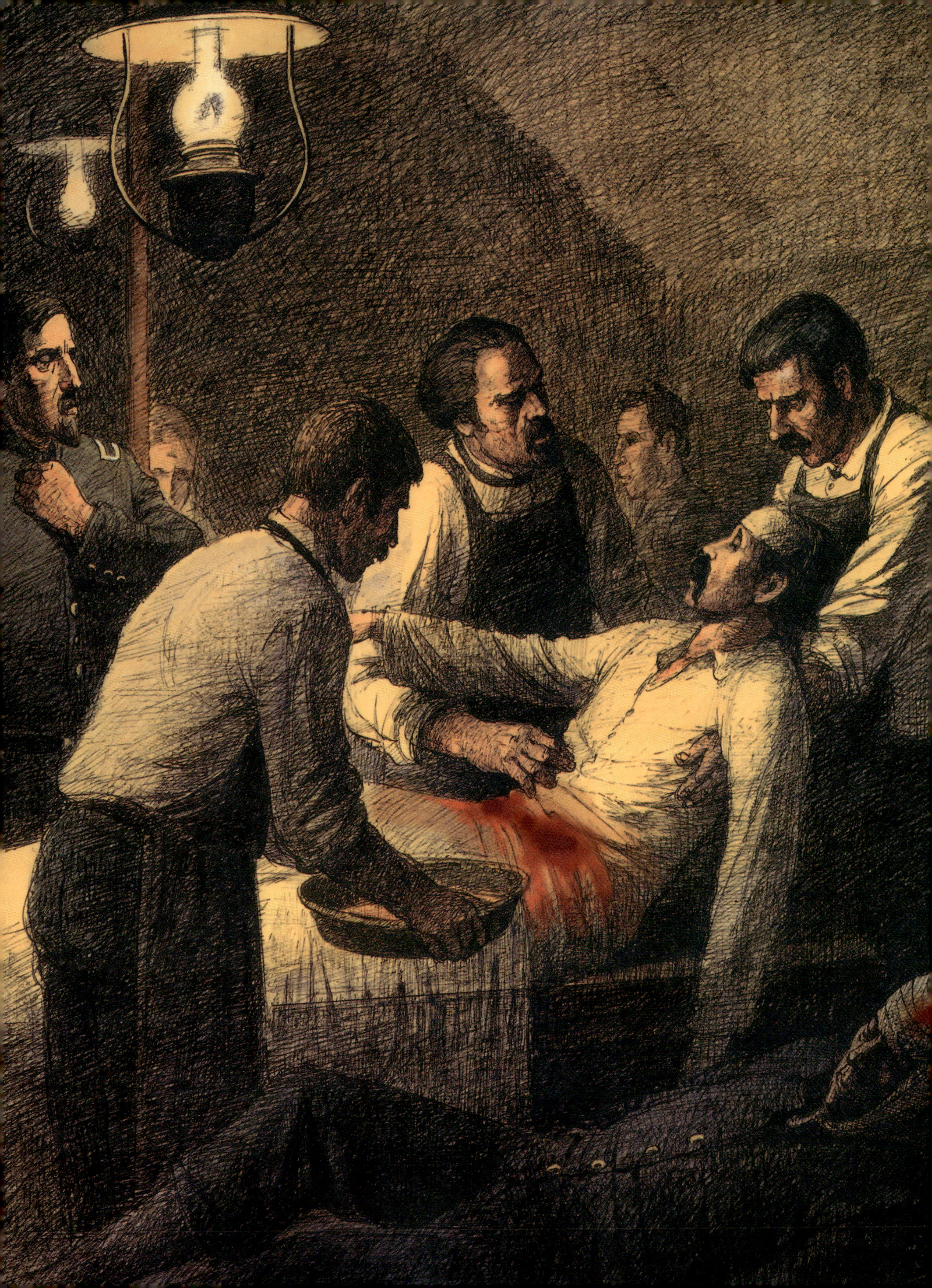

wounded. They ignored his order. At the field hospital, the surgeon said that Joshua could not survive. His officers and commanders gathered in the hospital tent to bid him good-bye. General Grant gave him a deathbed promotion to brigadier general. It was the only battlefield promotion that Grant ever gave. The newspapers printed Joshua's obituary.

But doctors cared for him in field tents and hospitals for five months, and, thanks to his unconquerable spirit and will to live, Joshua made a miraculous recovery. His wife and family begged him to retire from the army, but in November, though unable to walk a hundred yards or mount his horse unassisted, he reported for duty.

8.
VICTORY AT WHITE OAK ROAD

THE UNION CHARGE AT RIVES' SALIENT HAD, of course, failed, and the Union army began a one-year siege of Petersburg. In late March 1865, just after Joshua returned to his post, General Grant ordered a second attempt to take Petersburg. Joshua, now a brigadier general, again led the Union center. This time they would charge the Confederate fortification southwest of the city, along White Oak Road. Sword raised, Joshua ordered the charge. Charlemagne, his hot-blooded warhorse, smoking at a gallop, got well ahead of the troops. A bullet penetrated Charlemagne's neck and then passed through Joshua's bridle arm and slammed against his chest, knocking him unconscious. His life was saved only by a brass-backed field mirror in his breast pocket that prevented the shot from reaching his heart. The diverted bullet traveled around Joshua's body, inside his coat and out the back seam, striking Joshua's aide, Lieutenant Vogel, and knocking him off his horse. General Griffin galloped over to Joshua, who was slumped unconscious on

Charlemagne's neck. Griffin grabbed him around the hip to save him from falling. "My dear friend," he asked Joshua, "are you gone?"

Waking up at that moment and still groggy, Joshua thought General Griffin was asking him whether his charge had failed. He looked across the battlefield and saw that, sure enough, the Pennsylvania regiments on the army's right flank were in retreat before a Rebel counterattack. The Pennsylvania officers had been killed by a deadly volley of musket fire, and without leadership, the brave Pennsylvania veterans were fleeing. Without answering General Griffin, Joshua dashed off on the bleeding Charlemagne to shore up the line. Though he had no business in that part of the field, he flew toward the Pennsylvanians at full gallop down the center of the battlefield between the two armies. Bullets from both sides whizzed around him, and artillery shells pummeled the earth on every side. The ground shivered; dirt flew from Charlemagne's hooves; and a thousand Confederate infantrymen and sharpshooters fired their muskets at Joshua, hoping to knock the Yankee general off his horse.

When he reached the Pennsylvanians, Joshua, drenched in blood—his own and Charlemagne's—waved his sword wildly as he dashed back and forth before the Confederate lines, calling the retreating Pennsylvanians back to the battle. Inspired by this wild spectacle, the Pennsylvanians turned and rallied behind the bloodied general. They threw themselves savagely upon their attackers, driving the Rebels back behind their barricades.

Satisfied with this result, Joshua galloped back toward his proper position in the center of the line. As he rode across the battlefield, again in full view of both lines, the Union troops erupted in wild cheers for his spectacular show of courage. Then, for a moment, the battle stopped completely as Confederate soldiers climbed atop their barricades, doffed their hats, and joined the Yankees, loudly cheering the gallant Yankee general.

Back in place in the center, Joshua sent his wounded horse to the rear and continued to lead his men against the enemy on foot. Once again, he got ahead of his troops. In his excitement, Joshua crossed the Confederate lines and landed amid a group of Rebel soldiers, who surrounded him, pointing their rifles and demanding his surrender. Quick thinking saved Joshua from Confederate prison. Realizing that his battle-faded blue coat had been stained gray by gun smoke and dust, he pretended to be a Confederate general. Putting on his best Southern drawl, he shouted, "Surrender? Don't you see them Yankees upon us?" He waved his sword to signal his captors to follow him in a charge on the Yankees. Fooled by his accent, the Confederate soldiers followed Joshua into the hands of his men, and they were captured.

Joshua's actions at White Oak Road had turned a Union defeat into a resounding victory and broke the Confederate hold on Petersburg. He was promoted to the rank of major general for his gallantry.

In the next twenty-four hours, although wounded through the arm, Joshua would lead and direct his troops at three more battles, at Quaker Road, Gravely Run, and Five Forks, with no sleep: leading charges, enduring new wounds, crawling in the mud, dashing across

hot battlefields on foot and on horseback and capturing thousands of prisoners. At Five Forks, another horse would be shot out from beneath him. Union victories in these battles destroyed General Lee's flank and forced the Confederates to flee Petersburg. A reporter from New World Press who witnessed the battles called Joshua the "hero of Quaker Road, Gravely Run and Five Forks." Afterward, Joshua, now in charge of a division of 10,000 men, joined the pursuit of Lee's broken army.

9.
APPOMATTOX

FOR TWELVE DAYS OF FORCED MARCHES with little food or sleep, Joshua and his men chased Lee and his soldiers as the Confederates tried to flee to North Carolina. The bluecoats finally trapped Lee at Appomattox. There, in a narrow valley, the two armies faced each other: 110,000 Union soldiers against fewer than 28,000 ragged Rebels who could still fight for the South.

As Joshua surveyed the awesome scene, he saw three officers on horseback break from the Confederate lines and trot toward him, carrying a white flag of truce. When they got closer, he could see that their flag was a towel. They told Joshua that their army was ready to surrender, and that General Lee wanted to discuss terms with General Grant.

It was a stupendous moment. Joshua knew that five bloody years of war were finally ended. America was saved. Slavery was abolished. The cause for which he had suffered and risked his life and watched so many close friends die had been won. Joshua had survived and could now return to his family and his beloved state of Maine. Yet, all he could think about at that moment was to wonder, after months of continuous fighting in the mud, where in the world the Rebels had found that clean white towel.

After the terms of surrender were signed on April 9, General Grant chose Joshua to perform the task of accepting the formal surrender of the Confederate army on April 12, 1865. This was Grant's way of recognizing Joshua's bravery and the important role he had played in securing the Union victory. At the ceremony, Joshua took special care to spare the Confederates humiliation. It was a cool, wet day. The Union army formed lines on the road leading to Appomattox Court House to watch the ragged gray Confederate column trudge toward them to surrender. As the defeated Rebels lined up before him, Chamberlain called his men to attention and ordered them to salute their former enemies. At the head of the Confederate column, a sad General John Gordon heard the shifting of weapons and recognized the honor. He rose in his saddle, reined in his horse, and boldly returned the salute. Thanks to Joshua, the final act of the terrible war was a gesture of compassion and mutual respect. Tales of Joshua's kindness spread like wildfire in the South and made him very popular among his former foe.

After the war, Joshua returned to Maine to teach at his beloved Bowdoin College. In 1866, he was drafted by the Republican Party to run for governor of Maine. He was elected with the largest majority in the state's history and served four terms. He left politics to become president of Bowdoin College, and he died a hero in 1914 at the age of eighty-five.

Joshua was present at the second birth of our great nation. Indeed, he played a major role in the painful birthing process. Over the course of three years, he commanded troops in twenty-four battles and countless skirmishes. He was wounded six times. Six horses were shot out from under him. His soldiers captured 2,700 prisoners and eight battle flags. Before the war, this citizen soldier was a noble epitome of America's greatest virtues and the highest aspirations of mankind. During our nation's greatest crisis, he was a model for the courage, character, perseverance, and idealism that, for many generations, have defined the American people in the eyes of the world.

General Joshua L. Chamberlain, 1914

*"The inspiration of a noble cause involving human interests wide and far, enables men to do things they did not dream themselves capable of before, and which they were not capable of alone. The consciousness of belonging, vitally, to something beyond individuality; of being part of a personality that reaches we know not where, in space and time, greatens the heart to the limits of the soul's ideal, and builds out the supreme of character."**

QUOTATION SOURCES

Quotations were taken from *In the Hands of Providence: Joshua L. Chamberlain and the American Civil War* by Alice Rains Trulock, University of North Carolina Press, 1992.

*Page 4: Excerpt from a letter to Governor Washburn, July 14, 1862

*Page 5: From a speech given by Chamberlain to the members of the army of the Potomac Association, 1869

*Page 15: From "Through Blood and Fire at Gettysburg," a collection of Chamberlain's private Civil War papers, first published in *Hearst's Magazine* in 1913

*Page 24: Excerpts from a letter to Chamberlain's seven-year-old daughter Daisy, May 1863

*Page 37: From "The State, the Nation, and the People," an address given at the dedication of the 20th Maine Monuments at Gettysburg, October 3, 1889

BIBLIOGRAPHY

Foote, Shelby. *The Civil War: A Narrative, Vol.1, Fort Sumter to Perryville.* New York: Random House, 1958.

———. *The Civil War: A Narrative, Vol. 2, Fredericksburg to Meridian.* New York: Random House, 1963.

———. *The Civil War: A Narrative, Vol. 3, Red River to Appomattox.* New York: Random House, 1974.

Longacre, Edward G. *Joshua Chamberlain: The Soldier and the Man.* New York: Da Capo Press, 2003.

SUGGESTED READING

Shaara, Jeff. *Jeff Shaara's Civil War Battlefields: Discovering America's Hallowed Ground.* New York: Random House, 2006.

Shaara, Michael. *The Killer Angels.* New York: David McKay Publications, 1974.

ACKNOWLEDGMENTS

My gratitude to my extraordinarily talented researcher Brendan DeMelle, and to Mary Beth Postman, who organizes my life so that I have time to read history and write books for children, and to my assistant Lori Morash, who can somehow read my chicken scratch, and to Donna Bray at Hyperion, who helps to make this endeavor so fun.

Box Set Edition 2026

Sky Pony Press books may be purchased in bulk at special discounts for sales promotion, corporate gifts, fund-raising, or educational purposes. Special editions can also be created to specifications. For details, contact the Special Sales Department, Sky Pony Press, 307 Fifth Avenue, 4th Floor, New York, NY 10016 or info@skyhorsepublishing.com.

Sky Pony® is a registered trademark of Skyhorse Publishing, Inc.®, a Delaware corporation.

Visit our website at www.skyponypress.com.

10 9 8 7 6 5 4 3 2 1

Library of Congress Cataloging-in-Publication Data is available on file.

Cover design by Kai Texel
Cover illustration by Dennis Nolan

Print ISBN: 978-1-5107-8682-0
Ebook ISBN: 978-1-5107-7909-9

Manufactured in China, January 2026
This product conforms to CPSIA 2008

ROBERT SMALLS
AMERICAN HERO

ROBERT F. KENNEDY, JR.

Illustrations by Patrick Faricy

Sky Pony Press
New York

To my friend John Lewis and the other
old warhorses who never stop fighting for the
noble ideal of Robert Smalls' America.
— Robert F. Kennedy, Jr.

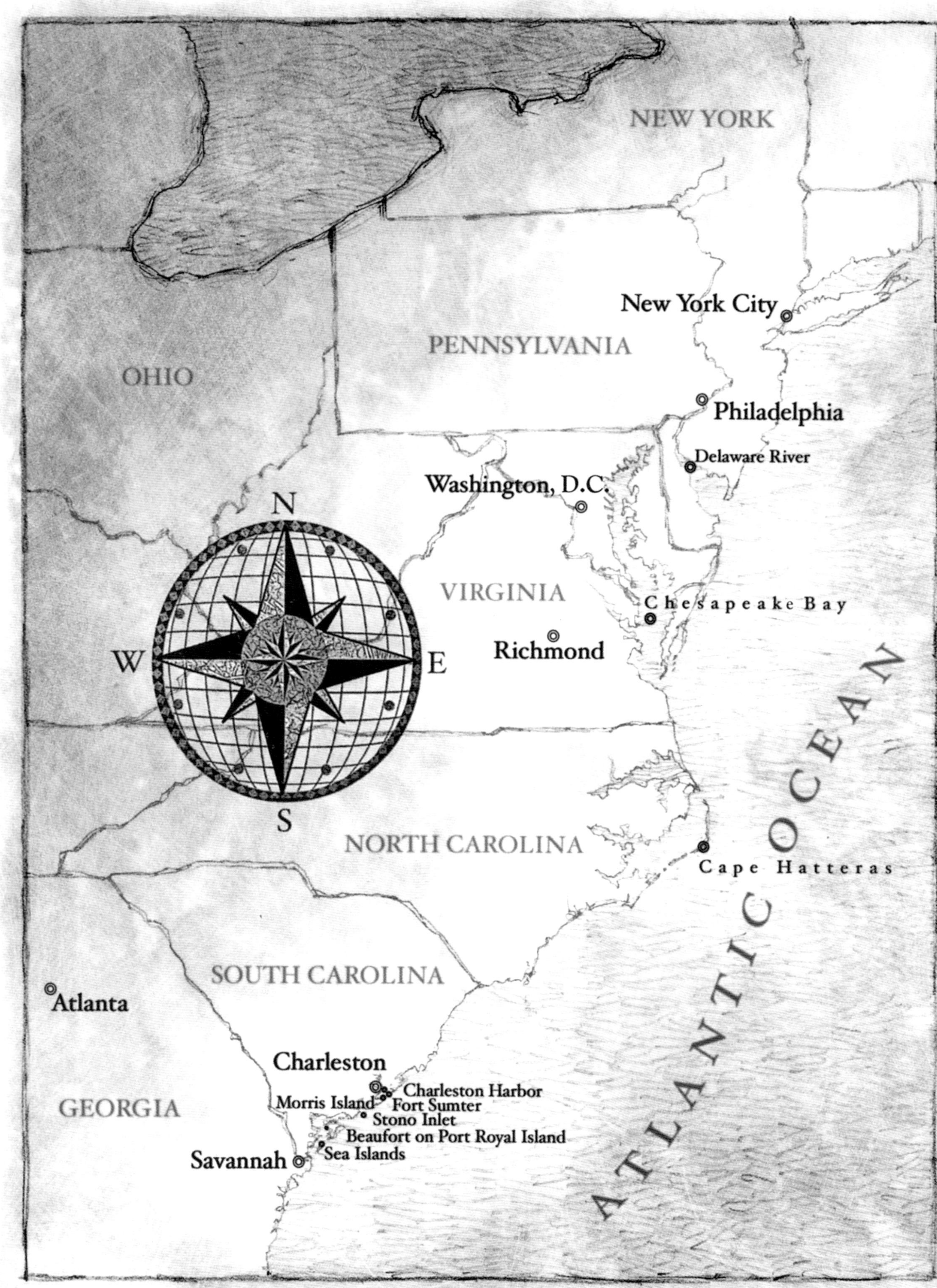

NEW YORK
New York City
PENNSYLVANIA
OHIO
Philadelphia
Delaware River
Washington, D.C.
N
W
E
S
VIRGINIA
Chesapeake Bay
Richmond
NORTH CAROLINA
Cape Hatteras
ATLANTIC OCEAN
SOUTH CAROLINA
Atlanta
Charleston
Charleston Harbor
Morris Island
Fort Sumter
Stono Inlet
Beaufort on Port Royal Island
Sea Islands
Savannah
GEORGIA

CONTENTS

Introduction / vii

1 House Slave and Sailor / 1

2 The *Planter* / 5

3 Sailing to Freedom / 9

4 Back on Shore / 15

5 The Battle for Stono Inlet / 17

6 Captain Robert Smalls / 20

7 Abe Lincoln / 25

8 Philadelphia / 28

9 Home to Beaufort / 30

10 The Confederacy Rises Again / 34

Afterword / 39

Bibliography / 40

INTRODUCTION

In the spring of 1862, the world was watching the South Carolina port of Charleston. One year earlier, the Confederate bombardment of Fort Sumter had launched the American Civil War. Confederate forces now occupied Fort Sumter and the many fortified islands guarding the Rebel harbor. The Union had enjoyed very little good news since the Confederate seizure of Charleston.

Then, on a moonlit May night, nine Black slaves, in a daring gambit, stole the Confederate's prize gunship as it lay tied to the wharf in front of Confederate headquarters in Charleston Harbor and ran the port's heavily armed gauntlet of outer fortifications and battlements, delivering the vessel to the American navy. The warship, a giant side-wheel steamer called the *Planter*, was the fastest ship in the harbor. She was the pride of Charleston and the most important ship in the local Rebel fleet. The daring slaves had commandeered her from under the noses of twenty-one Confederate troops guarding her from just a few feet away.

The brassy getaway riveted the globe and enraged the Confederate government. The loss of their finest ship, with its irreplaceable cannons and ordnance, was both a military disaster and a humiliating blow to Rebel morale. Even worse, the audacious and intricately coordinated escape exploded the Confederate claim that Southern slaves did not crave freedom and were incapable of decisive and deliberate action.

The bold feat of intricate planning and courageous execution at the birthplace of the Civil War electrified Northern states weary from the parade of grim battlefield dispatches. Northern papers praised "the audacious Africans" for their gallantry. The *New York Times* proclaimed the deed "one of the most heroic acts of the war." The plot's ringleader—an illiterate slave sailor named Robert Smalls—became a national hero. Editorial pages argued that Smalls had proven that Black slaves were ready for full freedom and citizenship. The *New York Daily Tribune* asked, "What White man has made a bolder dash or won a richer prize in the teeth of such perils during the war?" The paper added that Smalls' actions had demonstrated that "Negro slaves have skill and courage. They will risk their lives for liberty."

The daring venture shattered widespread stereotypes about African slaves and inspired the broad public support that allowed President Abraham Lincoln to issue the Emancipation Proclamation, freeing the slaves with full United States citizenship.

Both North and South were ravenous for every detail about the intrepid slave, Robert Smalls, who masterminded the daredevil escapade. This is his story.

1.
HOUSE SLAVE AND SAILOR

ALTHOUGH HE WAS BORN A SLAVE, ROBERT SMALLS WAS PROUD OF HIS heritage among the African tribes of Guinea. His mother, Lydia, made certain of that by teaching him that he was the descendant of great warriors. Lydia began her own life on a rice plantation in the Sea Islands off the South Carolina coast. She endured the most brutal cruelties as a field slave in the paddies until her owner, John K. McKee, moved Lydia to work in his home on Prince Street in Beaufort, a sleepy little city on Port Royal Island. Recognizing her high character, natural kindness, and sharp wit, McKee entrusted her with the care of his five children. At age forty-nine she bore her only child, Robert, in a wood-plank slave shack in the McKees' backyard. The McKees were among South Carolina's wealthiest citizens, and the family treated Robert well. When John McKee died in 1848, Robert and his mother became the property of John's eldest son, Henry.

Despite the comparative comfort of their lives as house slaves, Lydia always reminded Robert of the harsh conditions of her early existence. She made sure that Robert never forgot the precariousness of his condition by forcing him to watch slaves being whipped in the streets of Beaufort. She took him to the Beaufort Armory to witness the slave auctions. Robert saw families divided and watched Black people being bought and sold like animals, in leg

shackles and neck irons. In this way, Lydia inspired her son with an enduring hunger for freedom.

When Robert was twelve, his master Henry McKee sent him to Charleston, hiring him out as a hotel waiter and then as a lamplighter for the city. His reputation for being a hard worker landed him a job on the Charleston docks as a stevedore, driving the hoisting horses that powered the cranes used to lift heavy objects in the shipyard. Robert's good nature and ingenuity won him a rapid advance to foreman. Recognizing Robert's energy, resourcefulness, and technical abilities, the shipyard owner swiftly promoted him to sailmaker and topsail rigger.

In the warmer months, Robert manned a merchant schooner to the Sea Islands and the Georgia and Carolina coasts. He was soon navigating and handling every kind of boat with such skill and confidence that the ship captains regarded him as one of South Carolina's finest sailors. Although illiterate, he mastered all the elements of sailing. He could read maps and charts, and he understood the currents and the tides. Robert memorized the locations of the channels, bars, and reefs, and the bays and inlets from Charleston to Savannah, Georgia.

Robert's wages legally belonged to his master, but at age eighteen, Robert negotiated with Henry McKee to keep anything he earned over fifteen dollars per month. His sixteen-dollar salary left him one dollar each month for his own pocket. Robert earned extra money performing odd jobs and by the shrewd buying and selling of items during his coastal cruises.

In 1858, at age nineteen, Robert married Hannah Jones, a slave hotel maid owned by Samuel Kingman. Hannah bore a daughter, Elizabeth Lydia, a year later. Since his baby girl was also the property of Kingman, Robert bargained with the master to buy freedom for

Elizabeth and Hannah for eight hundred dollars. By 1861, after nearly four years of hard work, Robert had earned seven hundred dollars, an enormous fortune for a slave. But when Lydia bore him a son, Robert worried that the new baby meant that he'd now have to pay more to purchase his family's freedom. He began to dream of escape.

Robert Smalls had heard through the "slave telegraph" that his mother had been freed with ten thousand other slaves in Port Royal, South Carolina, when the Yankees had captured the island in November. She was now working as a paid cook in Beaufort for the Union army under Major General David Hunter. Robert was determined to move his whole family north.

2.

THE *PLANTER*

A YEAR EARLIER, ROBERT HAD HIRED ON AS A SAILOR ON THE *PLANTER*, Captain John Ferguson's high-pressure side-wheeler designed to haul cotton. Ferguson had chartered the *Planter* and her civilian crew to the Confederate navy, which had outfitted her as a gunship with a cannon in her bow and a howitzer astern. A large freighter, 147 feet long and 50 feet abeam, the *Planter*'s broad deck could carry a thousand troops and their gear. The *Planter*'s shallow five-foot draft made her ideal for transporting men and supplies through coastal South Carolina's labyrinth of estuaries, tributaries, and rivers.

As Charleston prepared for a Yankee attack, the *Planter* patrolled the harbor, placing mines and carrying troops and armaments to the outlying forts and batteries.

Soon after Robert hired on as a deckhand, his perfect knowledge of the bays and shoals persuaded the Confederate officers to promote him first to head crewman and then to ship's pilot.

One day, a slave sailor joked to Robert that they should steal the *Planter*. Smalls hushed his friend, whispering that the idea was more than a joke, and ordered him to never again mention it aboard the ship. After work, the two men began feeling out the other Black crew members: two engineers and four other sailors and deckhands. They decided not to include one of the slaves, a fifth deckhand, who nobody trusted.

The slaves gathered late at night to plan their dangerous scheme by candlelight at Robert's house. They agreed to be ready at a moment's notice and left it to Robert to decide when to move. All the conspirators promised to obey his orders.

On some nights the *Planter*'s White officers would leave their ship in Smalls' care, moored to the wharf adjacent to Confederate headquarters. Twenty-one marines stood on the pier tightly guarding the *Planter*. On the afternoon of May 12, 1862, Confederate soldiers and stevedores loaded the steamship with six heavy guns and several hundred pounds of ammunition for shipment to the harbor fortifications. The guns included two magnificent cannons captured from the Union army following the surrender at Fort Sumter. Local ironsmiths had finally repaired the Yankee guns from the damage they suffered during the fierce battle, and the Rebels were excited to deploy the big artillery pieces for their own cause. Thinking to himself that these weapons would make a fine gift for "Uncle Abe," Smalls deliberately slowed down the loading process so that the cargo could not be delivered that day.

At sundown, the Confederate captain, C.J. Relyea, his mate, and his chief engineer announced that they were going ashore to spend the night. Ambling down the gangplank, Captain Relyea ordered Robert to ready the ship to shove off at 6 a.m. on the high tide. "Aye, aye, sir," Smalls replied. The moment the sailors were out of sight, Smalls spread the word among his crew to be ready that night.

The slaves sent messages to their wives and children. That

evening, as Charleston slept, two women and their little ones stole away from their masters' homes. Arriving at the port in the darkness, they hid aboard a merchant ship moored to a nearby dock under the care of a slave sailor who was a friend of Smalls' and who would join the adventure.

3.

SAILING TO FREEDOM

None of the conpirators would sleep that night. Around 3 a.m., Smalls and his men slipped past the Confederate marines patrolling the wharf and boarded the *Planter*. Robert broke into the pilot house and donned Captain Relyea's uniform, pistols, and his broad-brimmed straw hat. Before starting the engines, the slaves quietly swore to one another that if they were caught, they would detonate the ship's explosives, sink the *Planter*, and die fighting.

Knowing the captain and mates might return as early as 5 a.m., the renegade slaves fired up the steam generators at 3:30 a.m. The roar seemed loud enough to waken the whole city. Thick smoke from the stacks swept down onto Charleston. A terrifying eternity passed as the eight men waited for the steam pressure to build. They prayed that the armed Confederate soldier on the wharf would not sound the alert, or that the howling, billowing turbines would not tip off the captain or cause someone to sound the fire alarms.

When the pressure was sufficient, Smalls ordered his men to loosen the lines and raise the Confederate flag. Then he blew the *Planter*'s whistle to signal they were leaving the wharf. Smalls stood beside the wheelhouse, wearing the captain's hat and uniform with his arms on his hips, elbows spread wide, imitating the captain's well-known posture. Shielded by darkness, the *Planter* steamed slowly across the harbor to the dock where the women

and children were hiding. As soon as they climbed safely aboard, Smalls turned his ship and sailed leisurely seaward, passing six fortified Confederate checkpoints bristling with deadly guns. At each fort, Smalls blew the *Planter*'s horns according to the coded signals, which he knew by heart.

The tide was against them, and they did not reach Fort Sumter till daylight. As they steamed past the great citadel, Smalls fetched up his collar and pulled the straw hat low to hide the Black skin of his face. He pulled the rope, making two long whistles and a short jerk—the final code for gunboats leaving the harbor. The officer on watch signaled him to pass, and Robert, cool as ice, steamed at a crawl directly under Fort Sumter's steep stone walls and powerful cannons. In that moment of greatest peril, he prayed to himself, "*Lord, you brought Moses and the Israelites from slavery, safely across the Red Sea. Please carry your children now to the promised land of freedom!*"

As soon as she was beyond Sumter's guns, Smalls buried the *Planter*'s throttle and changed course, racing for the open sea and the Union blockade ships. Through the morning mist, Robert spotted on the horizon the silhouettes of ten warships from the federal squadron. Setting course for the nearest federal gunboat, Robert ordered his men to strike the Confederate colors and haul up a bedsheet he'd stripped off one of the bunks.

From the crow's nest on the federal frigate *Onward*, a lookout spotted the Confederate gunship corning at full speed toward them out of the fog and sounded the alarm. Thinking it meant to ram them, the *Onward*'s captain, F. J. Nickerson, brought *Onward* about to meet a hostile attack with his broadside guns. Just as he was about to order a cannon barrage, a sailor shouted that the ship was flying a white flag. Instructing his gunners to hold their fire, Captain Nickerson signaled the *Planter* to pull in astern.

Captain Nickerson was shocked to see a dashing young Black man wearing the Rebel captain's hat, dressed elegantly in a white shirt and Confederate officer's waistcoat, leaning confidently against the *Planter*'s gunwale. Doffing his hat expansively, the handsome youth saluted and called to the captain, "Good morning, sir! I've brought you some of the old United States' guns."

On the *Planter*'s deck, eight triumphant Black men were cheering wildly. When Captain Nickerson boarded the *Planter*, the exultant crew engulfed him, pleading that he give them an American flag to raise above their prize.

As they hoisted the Stars and Stripes, five more Black passengers emerged from the *Planter*'s hatches—two women and three children. Smalls' wife, Hannah, had tears of joy flowing down her cheeks. Raising their infant son, Robert, in her arms, she told him to gaze at the American flag. "It means freedom, child! Oh, Robert, it means freedom!"

Captain Nickerson greeted them cordially. After hearing Robert Smalls' story, Nickerson sent him to retell it to the blockade squadron commander, who decided to send the *Planter* with its crew of escaped slaves under Union commanders sixty miles up the coast to Port Royal, the headquarters of the Union army and fleet. Their families would go to Beaufort, where they would be safe for the remainder of the war.

4.
BACK ON SHORE

BACK IN CHARLESTON, THE CONFEDERATE COMMANDER, BRIGADIER General Roswell S. Ripley, was astonished that morning when his troops told him that the *Planter* had vanished from her berth directly in front of Ripley's headquarters on the Charleston wharf.

The Confederate troops who had guarded the *Planter* that night said that they had seen Captain Relyea in his familiar straw hat standing at the rail in the darkness as the ship fired her engines at 3:30 a.m. and then steamed off, flying the Confederate flag. The guards were not surprised to see her go, since they had been told she was scheduled to sail early.

They watched her land briefly at a dock across the harbor. Then her whistle blew, and she steamed unhurriedly toward Fort Sumter, where the officer in charge received her salute, and thinking her on guard duty, signaled her to pass into the outer harbor. Only one of the *Planter*'s original crew of nine slaves remained ashore. He genuinely seemed to know nothing. At first the Confederates found it unthinkable that slaves could have commandeered their finest vessel. General Ripley only accepted the shocking truth when, using a telescope, he frantically scanned the horizon and found the *Planter* anchored between two federal frigates out beyond the sandbars.

The Charleston press called the *Planter*'s loss "criminal negligence" and blamed its Confederate officers for "disgusting treachery" in allowing "one of the most shameful events of this or any other war." Fuming over the abduction in the Confederate capital of Richmond, Virginia, General Robert E. Lee ordered swift punishment for the guilty parties. Captain Relyea and his mates were court-martialed, fined, and imprisoned.

Tales of the daring takeover triggered weeks of celebration in Northern states. Congress passed and President Lincoln signed a bill awarding Smalls and his crew half the value of the ship. Calling Smalls' leadership "one of the coolest and most gallant naval acts of war," the navy's grateful commander, Admiral Samuel F. Du Pont, asked that a prize of $5,000 be awarded to Smalls and that $15,000 be split among the eight other men and two women who had played key roles in the adventure.

5.

THE BATTLE FOR STONO INLET

WITH THE YANKEE OFFICERS ABOARD AND SMALLS ACTING AS PILOT, THE *Planter* arrived at Union headquarters in Port Royal at 10:30 that evening. The Union fleet commander, Admiral Du Pont, was anxious to meet Smalls.

After retelling his story, Smalls gave Admiral Du Pont a book he had managed to purloin, containing all the secret codes and signals of the Confederate navy. The Confederate code book allowed the blockade vessels to decipher the various signal flags that were raised by the Confederate forts and batteries across Charleston Harbor.

Admiral Du Pont was astonished that Smalls had memorized the location, size, and power of Confederate fortifications throughout coastal South Carolina and knew the exact locations where the Confederates had placed their mines and torpedoes in the creeks and tributaries to foil Union attackers.

Best of all, Smalls reported in great detail the movements of all the Confederate soldiers and arms. He told Admiral Du Pont that the Rebel army had secretly abandoned its fortification, guarding the northern approach to Charleston at Stono Inlet. Admiral Du Pont recognized that this information would allow the Union army to retake Charleston by land.

PLANTER

The Union army, under Major General David Hunter, had been stalled at Port Royal mainly due to a lack of vessels needed to transport the army among the complex waterways of the Carolina coast. Du Pont sent a dispatch to General Hunter with Smalls' information about Stono Inlet. In his dispatch, he described Smalls as "a man of superior intelligence" and urged that Smalls' information be treated with utmost importance. Acting on Smalls' tip, General Hunter immediately began moving his army down the coast for a ground assault on Charleston. The *Planter* was a godsend to General Hunter. His army had been badly in need of a shallow-water ship. Here was the perfect craft for ferrying the army through the rivers and shoals of South Carolina's coastal archipelagos. And best of all, in Smalls, they now had a master sailor with intricate knowledge of the local waterways. General Hunter asked Robert Smalls to join the expedition as pilot.

Smalls steered troops up the coast for the Union navy and led three federal gunships across the Stono Inlet shoals, guiding the attack on the fort. His detailed knowledge of the sounds and rivers helped the Union army take Stono Inlet and establish Yankee fortifications. The U.S. Navy secretary credited Smalls with making the victory possible.

Unfortunately, bureaucratic delays by the Union army prevented General Hunter from moving against Charleston. The stall gave the Rebels the chance to fortify new defenses for the city, and the Yankees dropped their planned assault for the moment. Nevertheless, the Union victory at Stono Inlet proved a turning point in the battle for Charleston, and Stono would be an important base in future operations.

6.

CAPTAIN ROBERT SMALLS

DESPITE THE LEGISLATION SIGNED BY LINCOLN AND THE EFFORTS BY Admiral Du Pont to award Smalls and the *Planter*'s crew their fair reward of $20,000 for delivering the gunship, mean-spirited accountants in the Department of War, not wanting former slaves to receive such a "fortune," reduced the total payout to $4,500, with $1,400 going to Smalls.

If he felt bitter, Smalls never showed it. For the next three years he continued to serve the Union army with rare distinction. He piloted the *Planter* and other ships through seventeen naval battles, always displaying courage and daring. Each time he engaged the enemy, Smalls knew he risked far more than did the White sailors he fought alongside. He and his crew of former slaves would face brutal torture, maiming, and death, if they ever fell into the hands of the Confederates.

On April 7, 1863, the Union command gave Smalls the honor of piloting one of the world's first ironclads—the *Keokuk*—during the naval assault on Charleston. Although the Union attempt to recapture Fort Sumter failed, Smalls distinguished himself with legendary coolness during the battle. When the fleet stalled with its flagship run aground, Smalls guided the *Keokuk* around the stranded ships for a direct attack on the fort. There he came under hot fire from the Confederate guns. Cannonade blasts struck the *Keokuk* ninety-six times, with nineteen shots at or below the waterline. A shell burst damaged Smalls' eyes and killed his first mate. Despite his injuries, Smalls steered his crew to safety, unloading them to a rescue ship just minutes before the *Keokuk* sank upright.

In May 1863, Smalls was back on the *Planter*, piloting for a Yankee captain on a supply mission on the Kiawah River near Charleston. They were carrying ammunition to an isolated Union army division on Morris Island and bringing badly needed rations to the hungry troops. Within view of the Yankee soldiers, a Confederate warship ambushed the *Planter*, forcing her between three Confederate forts where Rebel gunners raked her with a withering crossfire from three sides. The fierce fusillade tore into the *Planter*'s smokestack and wheelhouse. Fire from short rounds splintered her deck. The screaming shells and smoke panicked the captain, who ordered Smalls to beach the *Planter* and surrender. Smalls defiantly refused the order. "Not by a damned sight will I beach this boat for you," he shouted above the blast. As the captain ran below to hide, Smalls took command of the ship, sailing the *Planter* through the maelstrom of smoke and hot lead safely to the Union battery. Thousands of Union troops, desperate for supplies, had watched her run the savage gauntlet. Now they awaited her, cheering wildly from the landing. Major General Quincy Gillmore boarded

the tattered *Planter* to congratulate its commander and crew for extraordinary bravery and seamanship. After dismissing the captain for cowardice, Gillmore promoted Robert to captain on the spot, making Robert Smalls the first Black captain of a United States vessel in the history of our nation. He served at that rank for the remainder of the war.

7.
ABE LINCOLN

EVEN AS HE WAS FIGHTING IN THE CIVIL WAR, ROBERT PLAYED AN important role in the emancipation of Black slaves.

In August 1862, at the request of General Hunter, Robert traveled to Washington, D.C. with the abolitionist leader Reverend Mansfield French. In Washington, Robert met with President Abraham Lincoln; his secretary of war, Edwin Stanton; and his treasury secretary, Salmon Chase. Smalls urged the President to arm the thousands of Black slaves who had been abandoned by their masters when Port Royal's Rebel population fled before the Union army. With charm and eloquence, Smalls told the President that former slaves were anxious, able, and badly needed to protect the Union-occupied regions of the South from Rebel raiders. His eloquent plea convinced Lincoln, and Smalls returned to Port Royal with the President's permission to enlist 5,000 Black men as soldiers in the Union army. Smalls had played a critical role in shattering the color barrier that had kept Black people from military service.

Robert was considered a prince by Black freedmen. They greeted him as a hero everywhere he went. Despite his inability to read or write, Robert became an articulate and charismatic public speaker. Abolitionists sent Robert on a speaking tour to raise money

at Black and White church meetings for the Union cause. In 1862, the Black community of New York City gathered at Shiloh Church to present Robert with a massive gold medal struck in his honor. The medal showed a relief of Robert and the *Planter* in the port of Charleston. The assembly praised Smalls for his "heroism, love of liberty, and his patriotism." Deafening cheers shook the roof of the famous church when he appeared with his wife and his little son, Robert. Standing at the lectern, Robert spoke with modesty, nobility, and confidence for the cause of freedom.

In May of 1864, a convention of Black freedmen and White people in Beaufort selected Robert as a delegate to the Republican National Convention, making him one of the first four Black men to serve in this capacity. But Smalls was still preoccupied with fighting the war.

8.
PHILADELPHIA

Robert's commander had sent him to Philadelphia to refit and overhaul the battle-battered *Planter*. Jealous of Smalls' success and speedy promotions, a small group of Union officers conspired to destroy Robert's reputation. They arranged that he be ordered to personally sail the *Planter* north unassisted. They were confident that the illiterate former slave could never navigate the impossibly intricate channels and strong currents of Cape Hatteras, the Chesapeake Bay, and the Delaware River. They fully expected him to founder his ship and then be drummed out of the service. Smalls, however, was overjoyed by the challenge and made the trip in just three days. Once again, he had astonished his doubters.

In Philadelphia, Robert confidently supervised the *Planter*'s refitting. In his spare time, he worked hard learning to read and write, a privilege forbidden to slaves under South Carolina law. Of the *Planter*'s six Black crew members, only one, John Smalls (no relation to Robert), the engineer, was literate. When a reporter asked him how he had learned to read, he replied, "I stole it at night, sir."

Robert continued working to support newly freed slaves in the South. With his customary dignity, he also struck a blow for equality in Philadelphia. Returning home one rainy day from the shipyard, Robert and a friend had just taken their seats on a city streetcar when a conductor directed the two Black men to move to the streetcar's outside platform. The conductor explained that city laws prohibited Black people from sitting in streetcars and ordered them to make way for White passengers. Smalls, instead, disembarked and walked home in the rain. That humiliation to the hero of Charleston received national publicity. The public outcry inspired Philadelphians to repeal the city's race laws. The "City of Brotherly Love" finally integrated its streetcars in 1867.

9.

HOME TO BEAUFORT

BY THE WINTER OF 1864, SMALLS AND THE *PLANTER* WERE BACK IN action, supporting General William Tecumseh Sherman in his march across the South. After Sherman's army conquered Atlanta and Savannah, Robert helped move Union troops up the coast into the Carolinas. The Yankees took Charleston on February 17, 1865.

When Charleston surrendered, Smalls escorted General Rufus B. Saxton into the city, where adoring mobs of cheering Black people greeted them. On the outskirts of the crowd, standing with a small group of White people, Smalls spotted his old boss, Captain John Ferguson, the *Planter*'s original owner. Pulling General Saxton through the crowd, Smalls introduced him to Captain Ferguson, a gesture that testified to his changed status and equality.

After the war, Smalls returned to Beaufort, and using his congressional prize money, he bought the old McKee estate where he had been born. He would live there for the rest of his life. Working hard, he became a successful businessman and acquired extensive property and buildings around Beaufort. But he devoted most of his energies to public service. He labored to build Beaufort and Port Royal into communities where both races could live together, prosper, and flourish. Robert joined the South Carolina Militia, and he was soon promoted to major general, the militia's top commander.

As militia commander, Robert distinguished himself by peacefully settling a violent strike by rice-field workers. During this episode, he no doubt recalled his mother's tales of the brutality of South Carolina's rice plantations. Robert negotiated with the striking workers in Gullah, the language of the Sea Island slaves, which he had learned as a boy. Gullah was a rich mixture of West African languages and seventeenth-century English. The workers told him of their terrible mistreatment and the cruelty of the plantation owners, who used a payment system designed to return them to the status of slaves. Afterward, Robert kept his promise to the workers by persuading South Carolina's governor to pass laws making such mistreatment illegal.

Robert built the first public school in South Carolina and became the leading advocate for public school education across the state. He was one of the founders of the Republican Party in South Carolina. This was the party of Lincoln, who, in Smalls' words, had "unshackled the necks of four million human beings."

Robert remained popular among both the Black and White citizens of Beaufort, and in 1868, Beaufort's citizens elected Robert to represent them in the South Carolina Legislature. That year, voters also chose Robert as a delegate to draft the state's constitution. The document granted equal rights to all South Carolina's citizens. Beaufort sent Robert to the state senate in 1870. And in 1874, the town's citizens elected Robert Smalls as their United States congressman. He served five terms in the House of Representatives, longer than any Black person until the 1950s.

While in the House, he authored and passed a bill requiring equal rights for both races on trains. Prior to that law, railroads assigned Black people the worst seats or forced them to stand. Robert also fought to integrate the armed services and to grant women the right

to vote. He used his political power to fight corruption and waste in government. He fought for fair elections and battled to reform the tax system, which favored the rich and punished the poor. Robert used his personal wealth and political connections to provide jobs and care for many poor people, both Black and White, including his former masters, the McKee family, who were now destitute, having fallen on hard times. For fifty years, Robert Smalls was the most powerful Black man in South Carolina and a fierce fighter for American democracy and for the rights of the poor, women, and people of all races.

10.

THE CONFEDERACY RISES AGAIN

Up until 1876, the Republican party, which controlled Congress and the presidency, fiercely protected the civil rights of former slaves in the southern states. Most important among those guarantees was the right to vote. Since Black people outnumbered White people by nearly two to one in South Carolina, many Black officials now held power in state and national government.

But former Confederates were determined to deprive South Carolina's Black people of their newfound rights and restore the social order of the prewar South. They controlled the Democratic Party across the South, and by 1876, they began gaining power nationally. At the same time, the Republican Party began deserting the Southern freedmen. The industrial revolution was spreading, and large, powerful industrialists known as "robber barons" were using their wealth to gain control of both political parties. Tempted by that easy money, the Republican Party embraced the great corporations, abandoned its idealism, and left the freed slaves to the mercy of their former masters. Republicans now saw democracy and racial equality as "bad for business."

The old-guard Confederates now busied themselves with the tasks of reversing the reforms that Robert Smalls had helped win for his fellow freedmen. White supremacist Democrats openly stole elections and threw out most of South Carolina's Black elected officials. To discourage Black people from voting, the Ku Klux Klan made lynchings, beatings, and murder a daily occurrence. Wholesale voter fraud marred nearly every election in the state. "We stuffed the ballot boxes," South Carolina Senator and former governor Ben Tillman would boast to the United States Senate in 1900. "We shot Negroes; we are not ashamed of it!"

Beaufort, where Black people outnumbered White people seven to one, was one of the last remaining pockets of Black political power. Because Robert also enjoyed the support of many of Beaufort's White residents, he was able to hold his seat long after the white supremacists had forced other Black elected officials out of office. Nevertheless, Robert was under constant attack by the old Confederate guard, who still referred to him bitterly as "the boat thief." The Ku Klux Klan lynched Smalls' supporters, threatened his life and property, and turned every Election Day into a circus of violence, murder, and fraud designed to keep his supporters away from the polls.

In 1886, after Robert had served ten years in Congress, white supremacists from the old Confederacy finally stole the election from him.

Republicans in Congress joined with Democrats to prevent Robert from regaining his seat. Robert's enemies also had him imprisoned on phony charges of taking bribes; the governor pardoned Robert and released him from prison when his supporters proved those charges false.

In 1895, Senator Ben Tillman called a state constitutional convention for the express purpose of robbing Black South Carolinians of the right to vote. Tillman intended to repeal the model constitution that Smalls had helped to draft in 1869 and permanently relegate Black people to second-class citizenship.

CONV
NEW
OVERTURN
CONSTITUTIO
NOW

Only six Black people attended the convention, all but one from Beaufort. Robert Smalls was their star. He delivered a series of extraordinary speeches at the South Carolina Constitutional Convention in an unsuccessful attempt to prevent the disenfranchisement of his race. Through breathtaking passion and intelligence, he nearly succeeded. His eloquent plea against bigotry and in support of America's promise of a truly representative democracy nearly persuaded even the hard-line white supremacists, who now controlled the state. A contemporary writer called Smalls "a potent force in the convention."

"The ringing speeches made by him were masterpieces of impregnable logic, consecutive reasoning, bitter sarcasm, and fiery invectives. . . . His arguments were simply unanswerable, and the keenness of his wit, the cleverness of his arrangements, and the persistence with which he routed his opponents from one subterfuge to another astounded the convention."

But in the end, Tillman and the forces of hatred were too powerful. Their new constitution robbed almost all of South Carolina's Black people of their right to vote and the other rights of American citizens. In South Carolina and across the South, Black people would not regain those rights until the Civil Rights Movement of the 1960s.

Despite those setbacks, Robert Smalls refused to stop fighting for the principles of democracy and freedom. He campaigned across the country against South Carolina's unfair and undemocratic laws, always appealing to America's idealism, her decency, and sense of fairness. He remained devoted to the ideals of an America that treated all women and men fairly, regardless of their race.

His noble character had won him many permanent friends, and he never relinquished his optimistic outlook. In 1890, he accepted an appointment from Republican President Benjamin Harrison as customs collector of the port of Beaufort. Robert held the post for twenty years. He managed the affairs of the customs office cleanly and professionally and left an impeccable record of honesty and good management. In 1900, Congress finally gave him the additional $5,000 that was his rightful reward for capturing the *Planter*. In 1913, Democrats took the White House and fired him from the customs-office job. He left without bitterness. Robert died two years later in 1915 and went before his Maker beloved by his fellow citizens. His funeral was the largest in the history of the city. Thousands of grieving South Carolinians openly wept as a Black chorus sang Robert's favorite spiritual, "Shall We Meet Beyond the River?"

AFTERWORD

Robert Smalls was a true American Patriot. Despite the burdens America had laid upon him, he never stopped loving our country. Smalls believed in the "inherent justice" of American democracy and in the principles espoused in the Declaration of Independence. To him the American dream meant building a nation that was a praiseworthy example to all humanity, reflecting the best of the human character, and our loftiest values and ideals.

He played an important role in making America—for a short time—a true representative democracy for the first time in her history. Thanks in part to his efforts, between 1865 and 1876, for a brief shining moment, America came close to achieving her promise.

In 1876, the forces of ignorance, hatred, and greed eclipsed that America, which had seemed so much within reach during the decade after the Civil War. Always optimistic about human decency, Smalls was a practical realist who knew that democracy and freedom could never be taken for granted. His life was a noble, dignified, and courageous struggle for those ideals, a struggle that only ended on the day he died.

But Smalls' spirit rose again fifty years later to invigorate and inspire the souls and voices of a new generation of Black leaders like Martin Luther King, Jr., who would finally guide America toward keeping its great covenant with history.

BIBLIOGRAPHY

BOOKS

Billingsley, Andrew. *Yearning to Breathe Free: Robert Smalls of South Carolina and His Families.* Columbia, S.C.: University of South Carolina Press, 2007.

Brown, Susan T. *Robert Smalls Sails to Freedom.* Minneapolis: Millbrook Press, 2005. (written for young people)

Cooper, Michael L. *From Slave to Civil War Hero: The Life and Times of Robert Smalls.* New York: Dutton Juvenile, 1994. (written for young people)

Meriwether, Louise. *The Freedom Ship of Robert Smalls.* Englewood Cliffs: Prentice Hall, 1971. (written for young people)

Miller, Edward A. *Gullah Statesman: Robert Smalls from Slavery to Congress, 1839-1915.* Columbia, S.C.: University of South Carolina Press, 1995.

Sterling, Dorothy. *Captain of the* Planter: *The Story of Robert Smalls.* New York: Doubleday, 1958. (written for young people)

Uya, Okon Edet. *From Slavery to Public Service: Robert Smalls, 1839-1915.* New York: Oxford University Press, 1971.

ARTICLES

Harper's Weekly. "Robert Smalls: Captain of the Gun-Boat 'Planter,'" June 14, 1862. See http://www.sonofthesouth.net/leefoundation/civil-war/1862/june/robert-smalls-planter.htm.